We first met in a draughty school hall in 1992. We went to different locations of the same school but we were the same age so we were put together for teams. Through years of competitions, dance outs, weekends spent at class, and sleepovers, we became firm friends. We were always competitive, but were happy for each other's successes, and supported each other when the results didn't go our way. We have grown up together, travelled together, and have those secret in-jokes that only other dancers could understand. We have shared all the important birthdays and milestones in our 20+ year friendship. It's true what they say - the friendships you make through Irish dancing are lifelong. It's a special bond.

We want to dedicate this book to our teacher, and the Patron of the Australian Irish Dancing Association, Janice Currie-Henderson. Miss Jan, as she is fondly known to many, is a strong and determined woman, who has devoted her life to keeping Irish dancing alive in Australia and around the world. Not only did Miss Jan bring us together and offer us experiences we would never have dreamed possible, but she always impressed upon us how important friendship was. As she used to tell her 'little fairies' in class, "You always have friends in Irish dancing".

Irish dancing has taught us so many life lessons - discipline, dedication, how to win, and how to handle disappointment. It taught us about setting goals and dreaming big - things we took with us through our school years, and out into the real world. The champions we spoke to for this book each had a story to tell - how they motivate themselves, how important mental strength is, and how important Irish dancing is in each of their lives.

We hope this book serves as inspiration to you to reach your dreams, whether that is first place at a local feis, getting a recall, or winning the Worlds. Remember to dream big, aim high, and most importantly, value the friendships you make.

*Louise and Elise*

# Drew Lovejoy

**UNITED STATES OF AMERICA**

There are many things that I love about Irish dancing. I love the music, I love the competitive aspect, I love the rhythm of hard shoes and the speed of a reel. But most of all, I love the community. I am very lucky because Irish dancing has given me best friends all over the world.

> *Try not to force your dancing. Prepare, work hard, enjoy what you are doing, hydrate and eat healthy, get plenty of sleep, and listen and trust your teachers! They really do want what's best for you.*

### How do you motivate yourself to practice?

I think of being on top of the box & having my teachers introduced onstage. I work hard for them to be proud of me and there is nothing like hearing their names & jumping down from the podium to give them a hug of gratitude.

"Champions aren't made in gyms. Champions are made from something they have deep inside them - a desire, a dream, a vision. They have to have the skill, and the will. But the will must be stronger than the skill." - Muhammad Ali

To me a good dancer has skills and technique but a great dancer has all the skills and technique, plus heart. When I see a dancer really loving what they are doing, I can't take my eyes off of them.

For me stage presence is the whole package. It's impeccable technique, amazing posture, looking relaxed, and a smile on the dancer's face.

# Melanie Valdes

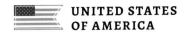

 WORLD CHAMPION | ALL IRELAND CHAMPION | NORTH AMERICAN NATIONAL CHAMPION | REGIONAL CHAMPION | BRITISH NATIONAL CHAMPION | ALL SCOTLAND CHAMPION

The thing I love most about Irish dancing is the amazing friendships I have made over the years. These are the friendships that I know I will hold for the rest of my life.

The way I motivate myself to practice is by picturing myself achieving the goals I would like to achieve. That moment when you win is the most incredible feeling in the world and is worth any amount of hard work. Also when I feel upset about my performance at a competition, it helps me to push myself harder in dance class.

One quote I really love is: "At any given moment you have the power to say - 'This is not how the story is going to end'." I saw this quote on Ciara Sexton's blog.

Someone who has stage presence will make the crowd drop everything they are doing and stop to watch. Stage presence involves having great technique along with plenty of stamina. Someone who has big jumps, a nice smile, and makes it look effortless.

*The desire to win inspires me. There are honestly no words to describe the feeling you get when you realize – "I've done it!"*

# Julia O'Rourke

WORLD CHAMPION | ALL IRELAND CHAMPION | NORTH AMERICAN NATIONAL CHAMPION | REGIONAL CHAMPION | GREAT BRITAIN CHAMPION

My favorite inspirational quote is, "I hated every minute of training, but I said, 'Don't quit. Suffer now and live the rest of your life as a champion'." - Muhammad Ali

If I could give one piece of advice to other dancers it would be to never let anything bring you down, not even if you are in the worst of situations. I have injured myself many, many times, and yes, it does take a long time to get back into shape; but all of it is a part of the journey of Irish dancing. You will sometimes fall hard, but a true champion will stand right back up. No one and nothing in this world is stopping you from standing back up besides you.

'Stage presence' to me is a very important factor at competitions. You might be a very good and talented dancer, but you have to engage with the judges and show them that you want it more than anyone else does, or else they won't pay attention to your dancing.

*The best piece of advice I have ever been given is, "If you dance your best, you've already won".*

# Brogan McCay ▮ ◗ IRELAND

I motivate myself to practise by setting little goals for myself. This helps me a lot because it makes me really want to do it so I can see how far I've come and progressed since I started.

My best advice came from my dance teacher Rosetta. I was at a feis and I wasn't dancing like my normal self, I felt very nervous and I found it very tough to try and keep positive, as all I wanted to do was give up. After my rounds were over Rosetta took me aside and explained how I could be upset and feel sorry for myself, or I could learn from this day, go home and work so hard that it'll never happen again. Those words have stuck with me and I can't thank her enough for believing in me.

One of my favourite quotes is 'Fall Seven Times, Stand Up Eight!'

One of my favourite quotes is 'Fall Seven Times, Stand Up Eight!' because no matter how many times you fail or lose yourself from what you love, you can get back up, try again and be better than what you were before.

My advice would be to never give up on yourself as a dancer.

You'll have more bad days than you'll have good days, but you have to learn from all of them because they both teach you how much you would go through to achieve your dreams and how much you love your talent. You might not enjoy training and the sacrifices you have to make, but it will all be worth it when you reach your goal.

# Amy Mae Dolan ■ ❮ IRELAND

I absolutely adore every aspect of Irish dancing. I love the actual music and dance style, the busy life of an Irish dancer, and the friendships. I feel like me when I go to dance class, practise or walk on stage, I just love every minute of it. I love the competitions, the adrenaline and nerves that make you even hungrier to win, and of course the glamour side of it, the makeup and the hair and the extraordinary dresses. I've always had a real passion for Irish dancing and I don't think that will ever change.

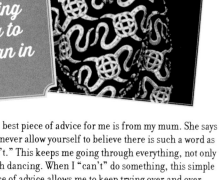

*There is no point in dreaming to win the Worlds or do something astonishing if I'm not willing to do absolutely everything I can in order to make it happen.*

The best piece of advice for me is from my mum. She says "to never allow yourself to believe there is such a word as can't." This keeps me going through everything, not only Irish dancing. When I "can't" do something, this simple piece of advice allows me to keep trying over and over again and to never give up.

One quote that I find hugely inspiring is "Happy are those who dream dreams and are ready to pay the price to make them come true" - Leon J. Suenes. This reminds me there is no point in dreaming to win the Worlds or do something astonishing if I'm not willing to do absolutely everything I can in order to make it happen.

You don't want to look back when you are older and think if I had worked harder I would have qualified for Worlds or recalled at Worlds, top ten or even first, and that's why you have got to do everything in your power to make it happen. Absolutely nothing is impossible, we hear this almost every day, but the best Irish dancers are the ones who do hours of practice and don't let anything stop them. Set your goal and be willing to do absolutely anything to make it come true.

I don't think stage presence is about your dress or wig or makeup - it's showing you truly love Irish dancing and about making the audience and the judges want to watch you. You have to say through your face and body language 'watch me!'

# Kevinah Dargan

 **WORLD CHAMPION | NORTH AMERICAN NATIONAL CHAMPION REGIONAL CHAMPION**

Being a student in college, it is very hard to find time to practice between classes, studying and homework. Whenever I have a competition coming up, even though I might be exhausted and just want to go to bed, I know I have to practice. Normally whenever I don't feel like practicing I think of times when I have had a goal and how good it felt when I achieved this goal at a competition. This makes me want to get up and practice because I want to experience this amazing feeling again and that would not be possible without practicing.

Before I go on my mom always tells me to give it everything I've got and leave everything on the stage, no regrets! When I am dancing and getting tired I always think of her saying this to keep myself going. I never want to walk off stage thinking, I wish I did this different or I wish I could do that again, so by giving it everything I've got and leaving everything on the floor I make sure I walk off stage very happy with what I just did.

> *My younger sister Fiona inspires me. She is always the one pushing me at dance; when I feel like I should stop, she is the one telling me to keep going. She is always so positive about everything, and helps me when I need it the most.*

# Fiona Dargan

 **WORLD CHAMPION | ALL IRELAND CHAMPION | NORTH AMERICAN NATIONAL CHAMPION | REGIONAL CHAMPION | GREAT BRITAIN CHAMPION**

*My sister is definitely my biggest inspiration.*

I love the feeling you get when you're on stage, the feeling of adrenaline. I love the feeling you get when you accomplish something you have put all your time into and want more than anything else. Irish dancing allows you to express yourself in a way like no other, showing your personality through every step on that stage.

My sister is definitely my biggest inspiration. She is always pushing herself to do better every day of the year, and always seems to love dance more and more every day. She is such an amazing role model and I wouldn't be where I am today without her.

Before I go on stage I warm up by doing single steps and stretching. After I'm all ready and in my dress I kiss my frog and bear, and rub my Grandpa's old ring for good luck. When I'm back stage I keep running my steps in my head and just moving around to keep loose! I like to talk a lot back stage to keep my mind from being nervous. It seems to work!

# Ceili Moore

 **AUSTRALIA**

I was once told by a very intelligent woman, "You have a sound mind, you have a sound body, and with that you can do ANYTHING that you may wish to do." This piece of advice has stuck with me forever as it simply reminds me how lucky I am to be happy and healthy and that with hard work and determination, I can achieve anything!

Just before I am about to walk on stage I remind myself how hard I have worked and positively tell myself that this will be the best I have ever performed before running over all the final details in my head. This tends to put me in a positive headspace so I am ready to perform. I also make sure I can see my mum in the audience before I walk on stage to give her the "don't worry Mum – I got this" look.

**"Follow your dreams, because you wouldn't want it so bad if you couldn't have it. The universe gives you these dreams because you can have them. If you're willing to work for it, you can have anything you want."** - Michael Flatley

# Danae Moore

 **AUSTRALIA**

If you could give one piece of advice to other dancers, what would it be?

Stay calm. You can't think clearly if you get yourself worked up.

**Walk on like the champion whether you are or not.**

My favourite dance is the reel. I love the beat of the music – it's fun, happy and full of energy, just like me.

*If plan A doesn't work there are 25 other letters in the alphabet.*

# Jonty Moore

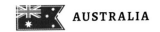 **AUSTRALIA**

I motivate myself to practise in many ways, but how often I practise will determine how much I want to win. For me, if I don't practise, I don't win, so making myself practise is crucial to my final result at major competitions.

My favourite quote is from Michael Jordan: **"I've missed more than 9000 shots in my career. I've lost almost 300 games. 26 times, I've been trusted to take the game winning shot and missed. I've failed over and over and over again in my life. And that is why I succeed."**

One piece of advice that I would give is to never slack off at any point when you are training. If you are training by yourself and plan to train for an hour, make sure you train for that hour instead of slacking off and finishing in 40 minutes. If you're doing a whole jig, make sure you do all 3 steps instead of doing 2 and 3/4. One thing I have realised over the years is that what you do when you train will reflect on your results. You need to make sure that when you train that you don't just stop because you feel like stopping.

Stage presence means to me that you look like you want to win or you are ready to dance with the way you stand on stage. If you look shy and unconfident before you even dance, the judges won't even look at you.

# Fiona-Gaye Moore

 🏛 TCRG   **AUSTRALIA**

**What's the difference between a good dancer and a great dancer?**

Someone willing to listen to corrections, take them on board, and perfect them.

From disappointment comes great success - I think this one often makes you dig deep and find a little extra in you to achieve what you weren't quite sure you could.

**What do you think is the single most important quality in a dancer?**

Resilience. Irish dancing is full of highs and lows, and the ability to keep believing, keep doing your best, and remember why you are dancing, is a great asset.

# Thommy Wilson

 **AUSTRALIA**

There are many aspects of Irish dancing that I love, but the main ones are the music, the ever lasting sentiment of being foot perfect, always having something to correct, and the extreme amount of concentration, determination, and perseverance it takes to be an Irish dancer. I also enjoy the idea of development and improvement that comes with Irish dance. I often find myself reflecting on my past dance experiences, and being refreshed by all of the bumps in the road that I have overcome, but also the path ahead.

**What's the best piece of advice you've ever been given?**

> *Working smart. It's not about how hard you work, it's about how smart you work, as well as how smart you can accept and defeat the challenges that come along the way.*

"Nothing is impossible, the word itself says 'I'm possible'." – Audrey Hepburn

I like this quote because of its relevance to Irish dancing. Nothing is impossible, if you work as hard as you can, and you are smart about how you work, you can achieve anything.

Apart from listening to your teachers and never taking for granted the time and effort they and your parents put in, work smart. Making sure you are strengthening your weaknesses without injuring yourself, not repeatedly doing it the wrong way, or getting into other bad habits in compensating for that weakness. However most importantly, never give up. Determination is an integral element to Irish dancing.

**Before I go on stage I do some last minute stretches, and I do some high kicks just to make sure I'm as loose as I can be. Then I listen to the music and visualise myself doing the relevant dance foot perfectly in my mind. I find this helps when doing it physically as you have seen exactly what you need to do.**

# Rose White

 **UNITED STATES OF AMERICA**

I love how Irish dancing ties me to my culture and family. That is a big part of what makes me who I am. I also love the feeling that I get after I know I have danced well - that is what will always keep me coming back for more.

"What lies behind us and what lies before us are tiny matters compared to what lies within us." - Ralph Waldo Emerson

When it comes down to it, dancing is performing and showing the world that you love what you're doing. After that, what is meant to happen will fall in its rightful place.

My favorite dance is my set. I dance to music that I listened to my family's Irish band play back in the day. It was always my favorite growing up. I always like to say my family is dancing with me when I perform it.

*My dad once told me "Do not dance to the music, dance with it. Because that is when you're truly performing."*

# Sarah Oldam

 **UNITED STATES OF AMERICA**

**You never get a second chance to make a first impression.**

Many people inspire me but I think it's the younger dancers who inspire me the most. I want to do well for them so I can continue to be a good role model and they can always have someone to look up to.

Stage presence to me is making everyone in the room stop and watch me. I want them to enjoy my performance as much I enjoyed performing it for them.

My favorite dance is definitely my slip jig. The music is so pretty I could listen to it for days. I love spinning and moving around on the stage. The slip jig is meant to be a very elegant and graceful dance and I try my best to succeed in making the audience feel I have achieved that grace while on stage. I enjoy dancing it so much and hope the judges and audience feel how much I enjoy it when performing.

# Gabriella Wood

WORLD CHAMPION | NORTH AMERICAN NATIONAL CHAMPION | REGIONAL CHAMPION | BRITISH NATIONAL CHAMPION | GREAT BRITAIN CHAMPION

I have to admit that getting myself to go practice can be difficult at times, especially when I'm alone at college. However, I tell myself that I would much rather go through the pain and fatigue now rather than on stage in front of tons of people. It is much more enjoyable when you are able to dance to your fullest potential because of the intense training you have done leading up to the competition.

My mom is my go-to person for advice and comfort. She always says the right thing at the right time. The best piece of advice she's ever given me is when she asked me, "Do you know what strength means? It means never giving up." She told me this when I was having a really bad day and ever since then, I've never forgotten how I felt when she said that. It was refreshing.

*"Nothing worth having was ever achieved without effort." – Theodore Roosevelt*

This quote is on my wall in my dorm at college so that I can be reminded of its meaning every day. If something comes easily, it's not going to be as rewarding as something you achieve with endurance and struggle. You must work hard for those special things in life. The harder the work, the more you will treasure the end goal.

I am so proud of my mom and she inspires me to never settle for what you have, that greater things can come to you every day if you work for them. My dad inspires me in the same way, but also by showing me that you can never give up.

Stage presence to me means that once you walk onto that stage, no matter who you are or what you've won, you are a champion. That is what you must give off, that you are completely confident in yourself and your dancing. I believe that a part of stage presence is not only your shoulders back and chin up, but also a warm smile on your face. It shows the audience and the judges that you are calm and truly enjoying your dancing. It's about putting on a show!

**Can you describe the feeling when you lift that globe at the World Championships?**

I wish I could describe exactly how it feels, but no matter what I say, just imagine it being so much better. It's like at that moment, you are being recognized for all your hard work that you have done in the past year or years. Sometimes people ask me, does it get boring after a while being able to stand on the podium or wear a sash or raise a trophy? All I think is, "ARE YOU CRAZY? No, it doesn't get boring! I wish I could do it every day!"

> *Ask yourself what are you nervous for? The fear of the unknown? Well hello, that's the point, it's unknown, so why would you be nervous about what you can't control! Enjoy what you can control – your dancing.*

Nothing is more rewarding than being able to stand on top of the podium, especially at the World Championships. The two times I won the Worlds, I remember exactly how I felt when I found out I won. I can re-live the moments in my head over and over again with specific details. It's crazy, but that just proves how strong the emotion is.

# Siobhan Casey  ENGLAND

**WORLD CHAMPION | ALL SCOTLAND CHAMPION | GREAT BRITAIN CHAMPION | BRITISH NATIONAL CHAMPION | NORTH AMERICAN NATIONAL CHAMPION | REGIONAL CHAMPION**

**How do you motivate yourself to practise?**

It's really hard, particularly after a long day at work and the travelling, but my teachers motivate me to try my best every time I practise.

**What does 'stage presence' mean to you?**

Confidence and obviously looking the part, if you look the part and feel the part it helps with your performance! If you feel good, you dance good!!

**How do you prepare before going on stage?**

I try to visualise my dances as it helps me prepare myself for my performance. I try to stay calm and enjoy every moment of the performance.

# Frances Dunne  ENGLAND

**WORLD MEDAL HOLDER
NORTH AMERICAN NATIONAL CHAMPION | REGIONAL CHAMPION**

**What do you love most about Irish dancing?**

Its history - the fact that it goes back so many generations is a wonderful thing. My Grandad had a school in Ireland over 50 years ago, so I really feel as though it's part of my roots.

**What's the best piece of advice you've ever been given?**

To always pick myself up when I've been knocked down. When you finally achieve your goals, the stumbles you've had along the way just make it all the more meaningful.

Don't underestimate yourself - no one got anywhere by not believing in their potential! Positive thinking is more powerful than you think.

Stage presence, I feel, is about looking as though you belong on stage. If you watch someone who emanates joy in their performance, then that to me is captivating. A natural smile goes very far!

# Nadine Martin  ENGLAND

WORLD MEDAL HOLDER | ALL IRELAND CHAMPION | NORTH AMERICAN NATIONAL CHAMPION | REGIONAL CHAMPION | BRITISH NATIONAL CHAMPION | GREAT BRITAIN CHAMPION | ALL SCOTLAND CHAMPION

Work hard in class and listen carefully to your teachers. Sometimes it can be hard to commit yourself to dancing, as it's really time consuming and can mean missing out on friends' parties and other functions, but in the long run it is all worth it. Sheer dedication and commitment is the key to success, and you will only get out of it what you put in.

I feel that stage presence is the ability to draw the attention of an audience, by the impressiveness of a dancer's mannerism on stage. Specifically for a senior lady dancer I feel that stage presence involves the ability to combine confidence with elegance, right from the moment they step foot on the stage.

Before every competition, my dad always says "Just do your best, but most importantly just enjoy it!"

I see slip jig as such a stylish, elegant dance and I love to perform it on stage. My light round is always my favourite at a competition, because the first round is out of the way and I find it easier to connect with the music and just enjoy the dance.

# John Lonergan ▪ ◣ IRELAND

It's so good to know if you do really dedicate yourself to something that you love, that there is a professional career out there for you. It makes it feel like now, after all the years of hard work, it is finally paying off.

The one thing I always used to motivate me to practise was basically picturing my biggest competition practising for hours. Kids these days don't win stuff by sitting around doing nothing, they kill themselves in class and work so hard. If I wanted to stay on top the only way to do it was to practise. I had no choice. If I wanted to come second or third or fourth etc, then I could sit down and just watch the top spot being taken away from me. That's just the way it is. You get back what you put in, so put in the effort and you will be rewarded in the end.

> "Never expect, never presume, always work hard & always be true to who you are."

The best piece of advice I have been given is to keep my head down, work hard, and get the job done. To me this is what I always think of when I'm competing, or even in show dancing. Every round (or show) should be a performance, and you must always remember there is an audience there watching you. Besides all that, if you don't want to win, or to lift that globe, then someone else is only waiting and would be delighted to lift it. That advice was the one piece of advice that always stuck out for me, and really helped me get through the tough and stressful times there are leading up to a competition.

"Never expect, never presume, always work hard & always be true to who you are". This quote really defines me as a person I think, and everyone can learn from it. As a champion, people think it's easy for me to presume I'm going to win, or expect to win, just because I might have been the champion the previous year. I think in the big world that is the "dancing world", people forget that the champions are only human too, and we, just the same as many other people get nervous, get blanks, make mistakes etc. It's only natural.

You can never expect or presume you're going to win, and if you do, then it's time to give it all up, or else question yourself and give yourself an awakening.

On stage, it is very important, for me as a champion, to be confident and to perform, but the minute I'm off stage, I'm back to my 'normal' self. Everyone is equal off stage, so just because someone has titles behind them, that gives them no reason to treat others in a different or bad way. *Everyone* is equal off stage, and it is very important to remember that. I always think of that quote at every competition or show that I'm doing, and it really puts everything into perspective for me.

My advice to other dancers would be to always, always listen to your teachers. At the end of the day, they are the ones with the qualification, and they will do their best for you, don't ever forget that.

Always work hard, and to the best of your ability. Whenever you're in class, you should be dancing as if you're onstage in front of thousands of people, not as though you're just in a class practising. If you do that I guarantee your performances will become ten times better.

> *One thing I will say is, have your inspiration, it keeps you working, but never try to be them. You're your own dancer, and never change that.*

As a defending champion, the amount of work that you have to put in is crazy. If you win it for the first time, and you thought you've worked hard, the amount of work expected from you the following year is ten times worse. It's so hard to get to the top, but staying there is the hardest part. Defending the title is probably the biggest relief ever. It's like a weight off your shoulders, knowing that globe will be coming home with you for another year. When you're on top of the podium it's just a daydream. I always find myself looking around the auditorium and just taking deep breaths in to reassure myself that it's real. People might think this is an exaggeration, but honestly it is like a dream when you're up there. To know that all the hard work, tears, pain, sweat, and just everything in general that you have put into going to the Worlds has paid off is just amazing. It makes everything worthwhile, and makes you realise that even though you might have doubted yourself, you have done it, and you're the best dancer in the world for that upcoming year. When I wake up every morning and go downstairs to see that globe in my living room, it just brings a smile to my face to know that I'm the World Champion of my age group, and I always realise how lucky I am to be crowned such a prestigious title. I wouldn't change any of it for anything, and am so grateful to everyone who has helped me throughout the years.

# Rohan Bole  SCOTLAND

**WORLD MEDAL HOLDER | REGIONAL CHAMPION |
GREAT BRITAIN CHAMPION | ALL SCOTLAND CHAMPION**

The thing I love most about Irish dancing is travelling around the world to compete, and the rhythm of the music.

When I'm practising, I remind myself if I work hard, I will achieve good results.

If I could give one piece of advice to other dancers it would be to never give up on your dreams!

To me, stage presence means having a good personality, being enjoyable to watch and looking as if you own the stage.

**How do you prepare before going on stage?**

I practise a little, tape my shoes, eat a banana, speak to my teacher, smile, push my shoulders back, focus and walk on.

> *"It's not what you do, it's how you do it."*

# Sinead Malone  SCOTLAND

**WORLD MEDAL HOLDER | REGIONAL CHAMPION |
BRITISH NATIONAL CHAMPION | ALL SCOTLAND CHAMPION**

**What's the best piece of advice you've ever been given?**

To leave everything I have on the stage.

**How do you prepare before going on stage?**

I fix my wig, touch all of my lucky charms, kiss my mum on the cheek and tie my shoes tighter.

> *"If you don't like it, change it. If you can't change it, change your attitude."*

# Paige Turilli

WORLD CHAMPION | ALL IRELAND CHAMPION | NORTH AMERICAN NATIONAL CHAMPION | REGIONAL CHAMPION | BRITISH NATIONAL CHAMPION | GREAT BRITAIN CHAMPION

If it weren't for Irish dance, I wouldn't be able to say that I have friends around the world. Attending international majors has given me a great opportunity to meet so many dancers that I otherwise wouldn't have.

Motivating myself to dance is something that I've never struggled with. I love to dance and I always have. To be a top dancer takes a lot of practice and hard work. There isn't a single day that goes by that I don't think about practicing. Of course it isn't always possible to practice every day but I always have a game plan for where my practice time will fit in my schedule.

It's the little things that make bigger things happen. If I break down my dancing and focus on - turn out at this part, pointed toes here, crossed knees there - eventually all the small pieces will come together to make my dancing even better.

Other Irish dancers inspire me! After so many years of dancing I still love to spend time at feises just watching the dancing. Other dancers inspire me to try new things and to keep challenging myself.

## It's the little things that make bigger things happen.

If I could give advice to other dancers it would be to first break it down and second, quality is better than quantity. The best use of a dancer's practice time is breaking things down and focusing on the small stuff, like foot placement and crossing. Breaking down your steps and focusing on the little things for 1 hour is better than spending 3 hours running your steps over and over and not having anything to show for it.

Right before I go on stage I think to myself that I would like to go out and entertain the audience. I've put the time into my practicing and now I'm ready to show everyone what I can do.

Having stage presence means having confidence when walking on stage. Many times I can tell who a good dancer will be just by the way they carry themselves on stage; their body language says "I belong out here." When a dancer has a smile on their face and they look like they are enjoying themselves you can't help but notice.

# Alana Pearson  ENGLAND

My favourite thing about Irish dancing is the confidence it gives me in everyday life. Before I started dancing and performing I was always a very nervous child, but now I have confidence in myself to try new things.

I was always more motivated to practise if my steps were more challenging. Every time I was unable to do a step, I was more focused that I wouldn't let it beat me so I practised, practised, practised.

The best piece of advice I have ever received was from my parents, who before every competition would always tell me it doesn't matter what happens as long as I go for it. They always said it's better to fall down because I've gone for it so hard, than stay standing and know I haven't done as well as I can.

**My teacher Hilary always said 'you're only as good as your last result' and this pushed me to make sure I kept building on my results.**

My inspiration has always come from my family. Their support has always inspired me to just do them proud. If my family are proud of me after a competition, then I'm happy.

Don't worry about the result - if you have danced your best and have had fun then the results don't matter. Irish dancing is all about having fun and being around friends and family, and that should be the main focus for all dancers young and old.

# Simona Mauriello  ENGLAND

I love the fact that Irish dancing has given me so many opportunities. I've been to places to compete and perform that I would probably have never gone to if I didn't dance. I love performing in shows as well - dancing in front of thousands of people without the pressure of results is some buzz.

Coming up to a major championship I find it easy to motivate myself to practise. I just think of a time when I danced at a competition and wasn't ready, the horrible feeling I got when I was getting so tired at the end of the dance, and wishing I had worked a bit harder. I want to go to a feis and know I am ready and that I can do my best.

*Rather than think too much about your result, just concentrate on dancing your very best, as that's all you can do.*

# Caroline Gray

  **ENGLAND**

There are so many reasons why I love Irish dancing! There is a great social aspect to it, I have made many really good friends from all over the world through dancing, and have also been privileged enough to travel to some amazing places. I also think that growing up in a competitive environment, such as Irish dancing, teaches you many life lessons. I have learnt discipline, good time management to maintain good grades at school as well as good results in dancing, and it also taught me to be gracious whether I win or lose.

Never worry about how any of your competitors have performed on the day of a competition. The only person whose performance you have control over is your own, and as long as you have done your very best then the rest is out of your control.

You can tell if someone has good stage presence if your eyes are drawn to them the instant they walk on stage. It could be because of the way they present themselves (as in hair, make up and dress), the smiley expression they wear on their face, or just a general aura of confidence about them. But whatever it is, it attracts your attention and in a big competition that is very important!

**Can you describe the feeling when you lift that globe at the World Championships?**

It was an amazing feeling, a moment I will never forget, and I am extremely proud and lucky to say that I have experienced it. I felt a great sense of achievement to know that all the hard work my teacher and I had put in had paid off and I was a world champion.

# Tyler Schwartz

## UNITED STATES OF AMERICA

I've always been motivated by taking baby steps. Sometimes big lofty goals can be too overwhelming! Making smaller goals makes it easier for me to make progress over time. Every time I go into the studio for a practice session, I push myself to fix at least one thing or make some kind of improvement. By taking baby steps, it keeps me from overwhelming myself, especially on more difficult steps!

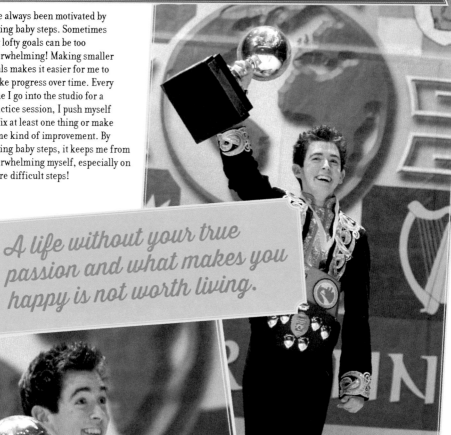

*A life without your true passion and what makes you happy is not worth living.*

A college professor of mine once told me "if you have a true passion for something, never let it go". I took these words to heart because I have such a passion for Irish dance. It's such a huge part of my life that I don't think I could live a life without Irish dance at this point! In my opinion, a life without your true passion and what makes you happy is not worth living. Those wise words will reside in me for the rest of my life.

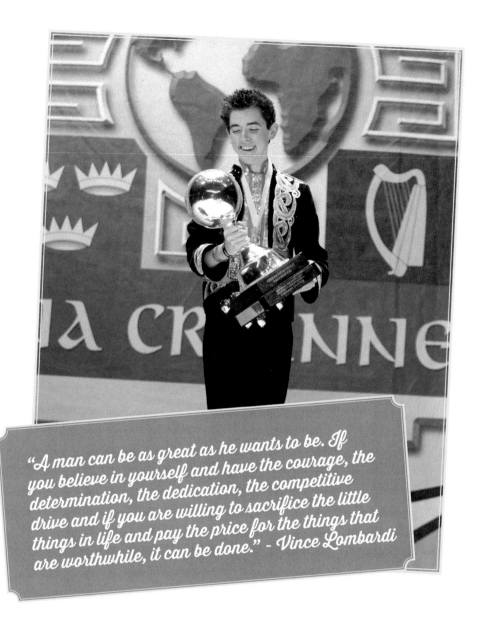

"A man can be as great as he wants to be. If you believe in yourself and have the courage, the determination, the dedication, the competitive drive and if you are willing to sacrifice the little things in life and pay the price for the things that are worthwhile, it can be done." - Vince Lombardi

This quote speaks a lot to me because I've always believed that hard work, dedication, and sacrifice is the key to become great at something. Everyone has their ups and downs in life, but the people that become something great stay true to themselves and dedicate themselves to the process, getting stronger every day. This is a lesson I've taken to heart not only in Irish dance, but in life as well.

For me, stage presence is another word for confidence. The judges want to see that you're confident in your own skin and you're confident with your dancing. It is also a way to set the tone of a dance before the music even starts! Stage confidence is also having fun and putting pure joy out when you dance.

# Peter Dziak

**UNITED STATES OF AMERICA**

I motivate myself by creating goals and then knowing how hard I need to work to achieve them. My teachers are a huge part to my motivation by pushing me to my limits each time I take the stage.

*The best piece of advice I have ever been given is that the sky is the limit, no matter how good you are at Irish dance you can always get better.*

My favorite inspirational quote is "What you put into it is what you get out of it!" and "The will to win means nothing if you don't have the will to prepare!" –Juma Ikangaa

The best piece of advice I could possibly give is to never give up on a goal. Once you set a goal don't stop working until you achieve that goal whether it be in your regular life or in the dance world.

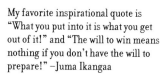

*Tyler Schwartz is a big part of my inspiration in the dance world.*

# Catherine Poulton  AUSTRALIA

My teachers in Ireland, Peter and Brenda Boylan, told me that I was not dancing for people over the radio – they said that I had great rhythm but it actually had to look good as well. I loved making great sound with my feet but when they said this to me, I realised that it was no good doing clever things and making tricky sounding noises if it looked rubbish. So I guess that has always stuck with me.

I am a school teacher, and every day I work with people who love what they are doing. As a result, the students we are working with learn to love what they are studying. It is the same in dancing – if you have a great teacher, they will inspire you to do great things. If they believe in you, then you will learn to believe in yourself. I have had some wonderful teachers in my life – both at school and in dancing. I think ultimately, these teachers have inspired me to do what I am doing for a living.

Ensure that you do everything you want to do while you are still dancing. It is no good saying five years after you have stopped dancing that you should have competed one more year or travelled overseas to dance. I would say to all dancers that if you have any inclination to do anything in dancing, then you need to do it. Once you are retired, it is for a long time! The window of opportunity for a dancer who is competing is so small in the scheme of things – you have to do what you need to do. That is an individual choice that will be different for everyone. But it has to be right for the dancer.

> My favourite dance was always my set dance. A great dancer once told me that your set dance is your trademark. That stuck with me for the rest of my competitive career.

To me, stage presence is having the whole package. That means looking good and controlling whatever you can to make that happen. There is so much in dancing that you cannot control, like where the other dancer will be on the stage or what the judges think about you. But there is also a lot you can control. Having the right tan on your legs is easy. Having clean socks and polished shoes for every round is easy. Having your make up, wig and dress looking pristine is easy. Walking out on the stage and having the self-belief that you have prepared as well as you can may be a little trickier, but it comes with practice.

I have often said to dancers that whether they are the champion of the section or not, they have all paid the same entry fee and as such, they all deserve to be there. They just need to show off and make it clear that they should be watched and that they deserve to be watched. It comes back to believing in yourself and your dreams. It cannot hurt to surround yourself with people who also believe and share these thoughts with you.

# John Whitehurst 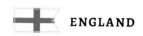 ENGLAND

**WORLD CHAMPION | ALL IRELAND CHAMPION |**
**NORTH AMERICAN NATIONAL CHAMPION | REGIONAL CHAMPION |**
**BRITISH NATIONAL CHAMPION | ALL SCOTLAND CHAMPION**

## *Winning motivates me to practise.*

The thing I love most about Irish dancing is the travelling that I get to do going to competitions. I get to see lots of different cities and countries.

The best piece of advice I've ever been given is to dance like no one is watching, and my favourite inspirational quote is "Do what you can with what you have where you are!"

**My teacher John Carey inspires me.**

To me, stage presence means showing confidence in my dancing and posture.

My favourite dance is the reel, because it's lively and I love jumping around the place.

# Tanya Cunningham

 TCRG     AUSTRALIA     AUSTRIA

The difference between a good dancer and a great dancer is hard work, passion and determination. A great dancer will put in the time and effort to achieve their goals, and won't stop until their steps are perfected. Like anything you're passionate about, you practise until you get it right.

A great Irish dancing teacher is a mixture of ingredients - they need to be patient, caring, passionate, strong, creative, and motivating. All the elements my dancing teacher Jan Currie-Henderson had while teaching me throughout my years of competitive dancing. Now as a teacher I try and contribute those attributes to my students so they feel as comfortable and inspired as I did.

I like to have loads of energy in my class to motivate my pupils. Sometimes I end up jumping around more than them, but I can really see a difference in their dancing when I'm running round the floor with them. I like to be full of life instead of just standing there telling them to point their toes! I also like to give little motivational speeches so they push themselves to perform to their full potential.

*I tell my dancers to go out on stage and put on a fantastic performance for the audience, or if they are nervous, I tell them to picture the audience in their underwear!*

# Janice Currie-Henderson

*God never forgets anyone – everyone has a talent at something.*

The most important qualities in a dancer are dedication, desire, honesty, self-belief, a love of dance, discipline and loyalty to their teacher. The difference between good dancers and great dancers is that great dancers are God-given, born with rhythm, well-shaped legs and beautiful feet. Great dancers give their mind to their teacher and do everything they ask without questioning them.

A great Irish dancing teacher must have a love of children, patience, kindness, self-belief, and a love of Ireland and its music and culture. The thing I love most about being an Irish dancing teacher is the beautiful children - whether they are champions or just little people who want to dance.

Before one of my dancers goes on stage at a major championship I say to them relax, enjoy yourself, believe in yourself and do your best. Don't be nervous

– dance for me as well as the audience. The best way to motivate your pupils is to love them and give them encouragement. NEVER criticise or put them down. God never forgets anyone – everyone has a talent at something.

The most rewarding thing about teaching ceili dancing is seeing the children give time to other people and work together as a team. The thing that sets good teams apart from great teams is discipline and practice, practice, practice. Brilliant teams dancers are not always champions at solo.

The things that have made my Irish dancing career so successful are a love of dancing for 70 years, a love of Irish music and culture, wonderful parents and husband, and family who loved and encouraged me all the way.

# Craig Ashurst

 **AUSTRALIA**

**What's the best piece of advice you were ever given?**

You cannot control what the judges decide for your results, so don't base your merit or self worth off what they say or what place you get.

It is very hard to keep your composure when you are shocked by a result or when you are used to winning a certain feis or big competition only to have a sudden drop in your placing. Losing is nothing to be ashamed of. In many ways, your humbleness can thrive because of it. We all take knocks, but I'm sure most people are aware that it's how you rise back up again that your character will be judged and your all round performance will be enhanced. If you can save your tears for the car ride home and give your fellow competitors the smiles and sincere congratulations that they once gave you when you had your day, then you really grow as a person. You become stronger and thus in a better position to bounce back to the top of your game.

> "Excellence is not a skill.
> It is an attitude."
> - Ralph Marston

Set goals, write down your teacher's advice and critiques for everything. Work out a practice schedule that you can honestly stick to and come back to class prepared with your homework done. Ask them for extra feedback if you are ahead of schedule and advancing quickly. Do not make excuses, ever! Be realistic with your goals. I would suggest not focusing on beating another person as it creates too much bitterness towards your competitors that could eventually consume you and ruin your performance for no solid reason. You may flourish more by striving to be the best that you can be and merely improving on that, time and time again. Always be positive and surround yourself with optimism.

I would make sure to eat really well in the weeks leading up to any competition. If you are snacking on junk food in your preparation for a feis or major competition, you are kidding yourself if you think you can progress at a steady rate. It slows you down mentally and physically.

I like to focus on everything that I've worked on in class prior to the moment on stage. Go through them as much as you can and visualise how it is you are going to perform. Make sure that you are well and truly warmed up and stay as calm as possible. A little bit of nerves is good as it shows that you care and you will give it everything that you have got.

From the minute you walk on stage to when you have bowed and walked off, you are being watched. Show them what you are made of and make them want to watch you.

> *Be humble in your defeats and never gloat upon victories. Always, always, always get back up again and rise faster, stronger, higher, bigger and better than ever. Do not ever give up!*

# Jeremy Heggie AUSTRALIA

## WORLD MEDAL HOLDER | AUSTRALIAN NATIONAL CHAMPION
## REGIONAL CHAMPION

The main reason why I love Irish dancing so much is the feeling I get when I dance. The adrenaline and thrill when performing is incredible and there is no other sport like it.

Imagining being on the top of the podium at Nationals gives me plenty of determination to practise.

"Listen to your teacher" is the best piece of advice I have ever been given. It may be cliché but your teacher knows what you need to do to improve. I was given this advice at a very young age, and my principal dance teacher, Jan Berne, is an amazing teacher. If you work hard to follow your teacher's instructions you will succeed.

**No one can succeed until you want to succeed.** A dancer must be willing to listen to their teacher, practise, but most of all believe in themselves. As soon as you believe in yourself, you will be able to surpass your expectations.

> *"Listen to your teacher" is the best piece of advice I have ever been given.*

# Natasia Petracic  AUSTRALIA

 **AUSTRALIAN NATIONAL CHAMPION**
**REGIONAL CHAMPION**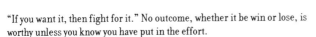

"If you want it, then fight for it." No outcome, whether it be win or lose, is worthy unless you know you have put in the effort.

There is nothing more inspiring than watching a special moment in someone's dance. It could be a leap, spin, click, whatever the move, when it is done perfectly, that is inspiration. Dancers aim to do better when they see something magnificent. This is what separates the good dancers from the great.

Discover what works for you as a dancer. Remember that everyone has different limitations; therefore play to your strengths. Once you find yourself within your dancing, the easier and more rewarding it becomes.

> *There is always room for improvements so don't ever feel that you should rest on something, when it can be better than it was before.*

# Leanne Halloran

 ADCRG  AUSTRALIA

A good dancer has technique, posture, rhythm, and turnout - all necessary traits. A great dancer has all of this plus the extra X Factor that connects with the judges and the audience. They are able to dance from head to toe. They are able to make it all look easy.

A great Irish dancing teacher is one who can teach the obvious necessary requirements of technique, posture, rhythm, and turnout but can also adjust the needs for each individual student. You need to be able to inspire and encourage through the correction and criticism.

I have often said to my dancers that they should go on stage to perform and show off and NOT to compete. Also I have always said to do everything with class!

I always encourage my pupils to understand that they get out of Irish dancing what they put into it.

> *Quality is better than quantity. I will always praise effort and hard work above ability.*

# Natalie O'Connor  AUSTRALIA

I have always believed that the rhythm of the dance steps is infectious and the sound that dancers can make with their feet is just incredible.

It's not only an athlete's performance that makes them a true champion, but their off-stage presence and persona too, and I believe this is what makes the difference between a 'winner' and a 'champion'.

*Visualising my dances in my head is always a good way for me to stay focused and prepare before I go on stage.*

The slip jig is a very feminine dance and must be danced with grace and elegance. I love the feeling of the freedom that I feel I have on stage when I dance the slip jig. It feels so effortless, like floating on air.

The feeling I get when I win a major championship like the Nationals is almost indescribable. It's such an overwhelming experience when you're on stage for presentations and you're the last one left standing. To be recognised as being the best dancer in your section is an incredible feeling, but to know that it is for something you love and have worked so hard for, just makes it all the better.

# Carina Young  AUSTRALIA

Irish dancing has given me the opportunity to travel the world, make life long friendships, and has taught me what you can achieve with hard work, sacrifice, dedication and commitment.

Honestly I have never had to motivate/push myself to practise, it is something I know I must do to get to the top and stay there. When I was younger I used to dance for Mum while she was peeling the veggies and cooking dinner!

*Listen to your teacher. When they correct your technique, do not take it personally – they're trying to make you a better dancer.*

My teacher has always told me to walk on stage with my head held high and shoulders back, as if to say "I'm here, look at me". You're always dancing on stage with one or two others so it's important to catch the judge's eye and make them want to watch you. If you believe that you're a great dancer, everyone else believes it too.

# Liam Ayres

 TCRG      AUSTRALIA

A great dancer has the ability to make you want to watch them. Yes, rhythm, technical ability and stage presence are all important individual factors; good dancers have a mixture of these. When put altogether and combined with a deep-seated passion, this is what makes a great dancer.

Positive reinforcements and the ability to keep the dancer enjoying what they're doing while constructively criticising are some of the most important attributes of a great Irish dancing teacher.

"If you only ever give 90% in training, you'll only ever give 90% when it matters" –Michael Owen

I love that what we do is so specific and requires so much dedication, that only Irish dancers can really understand it completely. I love that the Irish dancing community, as wide spread as it now is, can all band together with a mutual understanding and love for this incredibly athletic artform.

> *"Great dancers are not great because of their technique; they are great because of their passion." –Martha Graham*

Great teams have to be exactly that, a team. Each member has to have their heads switched on in the exact same place as everyone else in it. You have to be aware of not only your own position, but almost have 4, 8 or 16 pairs of eyes! Dancers have to be alert of spacing, lines and consistency, and also making sure everyone dances at the same level i.e. backwork, up on the toes, free arms in, etc. A good team has these elements, but a great team makes me want to watch them from start to finish and be able to enjoy their dance.

# Christine Ayres

 ADCRG     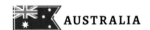 AUSTRALIA

Dedication is a very important quality in any dancer. A dancer needs to be dedicated to class, practice, and performing to the best of their ability at any feis, whether it be a local competition or a major championship.

I love the camaraderie displayed between the dancers not only within the school but the extended friendships formed worldwide at major championships. Team dancing seems to bring Irish dancing friendships even closer which in turn makes the team work well together. Great teams strive for perfection. The team members ensure there is a commitment to attendance at every class, working together as a team and practising at any free moment during class.

I love watching the new beginner dancers getting their first dance to music and seeing how proud their parents are. I also love to see the dancers grow and develop their dancing skills.

> *"To give anything less than your best is to sacrifice the gift." - Michael Jordan*

# Conor Ayres

🏛 TCRG     AUSTRALIA

## Great dancers make the extremely difficult art of Irish dancing look effortless.

A great dancer is the one everyone stops to watch, and can take people's breath away. A great dancer is the one who works the hardest to be the best they can be. They work with their teachers, and they inspire others to be like them.

**What do you think is the single most important quality in a dancer?**

Passion. If a dancer doesn't love what they do, how will they be inspired or motivated? Why would they want to practise when they don't really have passion for what they do?

Great Irish dancing teachers have passion for all their students, from beginner to open. They love what they do. How will they motivate their dancers to strive for greatness if they aren't passionate about Irish dancing themselves?

Practice doesn't make perfect - perfect practice makes perfect. A footballer once said that in a press conference when I was a child and it has stuck with me since. Don't just practise your dance, practise the parts you're having difficulty with and do them over and over again until they're perfect.

My other favourite quote is my own - Practise like you want it. You can't get up on stage and wing it. You have to work up to it. You don't want to get up on stage on the day thinking "Hmmm, maybe I should have turned off the TV and done an extra 30 minutes making sure I get my double clicks," or "Oh dear, I never mastered those back rallies I do in my third step...". You want to get up on stage on the day completely confident you have done everything you could have to ensure you dance your best.

Great teams are groups of dancers dancing as one. Great teams dance cohesively. Individuals in teams actively look to make sure they're wheeling the same, or that they're in line. If each individual dancer in that team is thinking about the same things, you have a great team.

A great team is also one that takes initiative. They work together constantly. They motivate each other. They encourage each other and communicate.

I love the fact some dancers who might not be the strongest solo dancers have the opportunity to be successful in teams.

# Julia Baar

 **AUSTRALIA**

*"Don't be upset by the results you didn't get with the work you didn't do."*

There is no point in taking part in something that you don't enjoy because you will just end up frustrated, angry and upset. Love what you are doing and never let the competition and craziness of Irish dancing get the better of who you are or who you want to be.

My favourite dance will always be the The Vanishing Lake. As soon as I heard the tune I fell in love with it. I believe The Vanishing Lake tells a wonderful story and when I dance to it I feel like the narrator.

When I first won the Australian National Championships, I was 11. It is still the best day of my life to date. I had trained incredibly hard for the Championships and taking the title of Australian National Champion was all it was made out to be. I remember I started crying from about 15th place because my nerves took over and it was all so overwhelming, and when it reached the top 3 places I could hardly control my body. I had placed 2nd two years in a row leading up to it, but I had worked that extra bit harder this year and wanted it so much more. When my number was called out as the Champion, I cried like a baby. It was the best feeling in the world, to know that all my hard work and dedication had paid off and how proud my teacher and family would be of me.

# Geraldine French

 ADCRG  **AUSTRALIA**

**What's the difference between a good dancer and a great dancer?**
The X factor - it is very difficult to explain why one child always seems to pull it out over another child who appears to be technically equal. There is an air about a great dancer who adds just some little thing to the performance. Perhaps it is just a way of holding themselves, or an extra amount of confidence that comes from inside the child, but whatever it may be it is an absolute pleasure to watch that child perform. Whether it be in a private class, normal class, or a performance in front of thousands, it is always there.

I've tried many things over the years to motivate my students, and have found that you never know what is going to work for every individual child so you just keep trying; when it works it is a marvellous feeling. Never give up trying to find the correct thing that clicks for that child.

**Can you describe the feeling when you win a major championship?** It is a very exciting moment, especially if it has been a particularly hard fought battle. But I must also add that some of the most exciting moments have come from students achieving their personal bests as well. You just never know what moment is going to be the best. I have been lucky enough to be the teacher of many students who won major championships, but I have also been brought to tears by children who made recalls for the first time.

**It is an amazing thing to teach something you love. And never stop learning - every child has a lot to teach you as the teacher.**

# Nicole Zepcevski  AUSTRALIA

I loved Irish dancing for so many reasons like making friends and travelling all over the world, but none of that compared to the feeling of accomplishment and self satisfaction I would get from improving myself as a dancer.

Being from Australia really motivated me to push myself 110% everyday. Before myself, only one female Australian had won the world championships in the 80's. I knew that the odds were against me and that I had a long way to go to reach the standard of my overseas competitors, but my desire to bring that globe back home to Australia really motivated me to be the best I could possibly be!

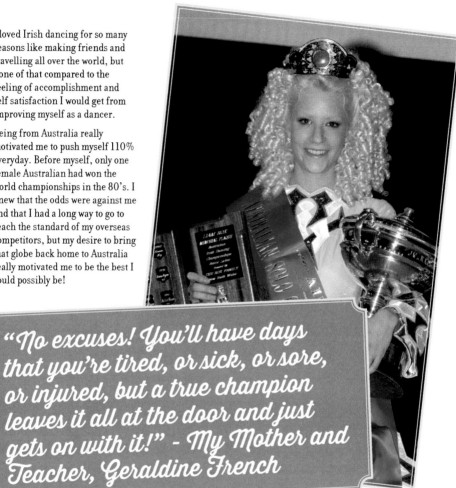

*"No excuses! You'll have days that you're tired, or sick, or sore, or injured, but a true champion leaves it all at the door and just gets on with it!" - My Mother and Teacher, Geraldine French*

**Can you describe the feeling when you lifted that cup at the World Championships?**

That was and always will be one of the greatest moments of my life. I had such an overwhelming feeling of joy and satisfaction. Against all odds I fulfilled my dream and proved to myself that anything is possible.

**Who inspires you?**

The underdog! I'm inspired by anyone who's overcome unbelievable odds or challenges and succeeded despite them all.

**Having great stage presence is to make the hardest thing you've ever done in your life look effortless and to make the audience believe you are enjoying yourself whilst doing it!**

**WORLD CHAMPION | ALL IRELAND CHAMPION
NORTH AMERICAN NATIONAL CHAMPION | REGIONAL CHAMPION**

**"Our doubts are traitors, and make us lose the good we oft might win, by fearing to attempt." -Shakespeare**

As a male dancer who went to an all male college prep school in the inner city that primarily focused on sports, I was not well received by other guys when I quit traditional sports to focus on dance. The hatred and jealousy I faced fueled my training regimen. I felt like I had something to prove to the world, and training hard every day to win was a way to silence the negativity around me.

A piece of advice that has rung true for me repeatedly is that no dream is too big and that positive visualization can help make that dream a reality. I used to study great athletes like Michael Jordan and Tiger Woods - both of whom had incredibly tough mental games to complement their physical prowess. From them I learned that the process of visualizing perfection and staying positive amongst tough obstacles is a major component to dominating a sport.

I would advise dancers to always go the extra mile when training and to focus on every single detail - when you think you have trained hard enough for the day, imagine how your competition is probably training even harder. That little bit of extra work can go a long way.

*To me, stage presence is your way of telling the judges, the audience, and the rest of the competitors that you are the one to watch and that you own the stage for the few minutes you are on it.*

# Melissa McCarthy  UNITED STATES OF AMERICA

Honestly, I love everything about Irish dance. The feelings of success, the strong friendships that are made, and traveling all over the world are definitely my absolute favorite things about dance.

When a major is coming up I usually don't need motivation. Just knowing that Worlds, Nationals or any other major is right around the corner is motivation itself! I never want to come home from a competition disappointed, so I use that to motivate me as well.

Stage presence to me means looking comfortable and being in control of the stage. Dance like it is a performance – not a competition.

My favorite dance is the reel because I love the fast and upbeat music along with leaping and twirling across the floor.

*My favorite inspirational quote is "Be so good they can't ignore you."*

# Layla Healy  IRELAND

**How do you motivate yourself to practise?**

Knowing that with practice comes perfection and that you only get out of something what you put into it. So the more I practise the better I can be.

What inspires me is being at a competition and seeing an amazing dancer perform and wanting to be like them!

Stage presence is to look confident, look like you're enjoying what you're doing, and wanting to be there in that moment.

**If you could give one piece of advice to other dancers, what would it be?**

Keep motivated, focused and PRACTISE PRACTISE PRACTISE! NEVER give up!

*I Can, I Am, I Will.*

# Mona Ni Rodaigh

🏛 ADCRG  ▮ ◄ IRELAND

**What do you say to a dancer before they go on stage at a major championship?**

You are walking on stage with 100 - what you walk off with is entirely up to you.

**What sets good teams apart from great teams?**

Dedication and hunger from the dancers.

**What's the difference between a good dancer and a great dancer?**

Talent, plus someone who is prepared to walk the walk and talk the talk, 7 days a week and 52 weeks of the year.

> *You never get a second chance to make a first impression.*

# Ciara Lennon

🏛 ADCRG  ▮ ◄ IRELAND

The actual teaching part is often the easiest aspect of being a dancing teacher. I think a great Irish dancing teacher should be able to bring out the best in each dancer, by instilling confidence and self-belief. A great teacher should also understand that no two students learn in the same way and teaching styles and steps, for example, may have to be adapted for different dancers.

My mam (Mona Ni Rodaigh) has a huge repertoire of inspirational quotes, many of which I steal when teaching! I think my favourite one is 'You never get a second chance to make a first impression'. It's so true, the numbers in high profile competitions these days are so big that it is vital the dancer strikes a chord with the adjudicator straight away.

The sense of camaraderie between dancers is one aspect I like in Irish dancing - I love seeing the children in the class work and play together. Seeing dancing friends 'of old'...! is also something I look forward to when I go to the bigger competitions.

> *Team dancing offers so many opportunities to dancers of all levels.*

I love that children who will probably never excel in solo dancing may be part of a world champion team. Team dancing offers so many opportunities to dancers of all levels. As mentioned above, I also love the camaraderie and the palpable team spirit when the dancers 'gel' together.

A great team is made of dancers who actually want to participate as part of a group and do not bring their 'solo' dancing heads to team practice. There's no 'I' in TEAM..... (another well used 'Mona quote'!). It's important that the dancers communicate and get on well with each other on and off the stage, looking out for one another at every opportunity.

# Dearbhla Lennon

 ADCRG  IRELAND

**What's the difference between a good dancer and a great dancer?**

Technical ability accounts for a small part of this answer. But without a doubt the key difference is a dancer's hunger to succeed. And not just wanting it, but wanting it badly enough to be willing to put the work in morning, noon and night. Willing to make the kind of sacrifices necessary to make you better, possibly even make you the best.

*It's no good making half the practices - a team needs to be unbelievably dedicated to succeed.*

There are a couple of things that I feel make a teacher great. The first would be a true understanding of and passion for the art form. The second would be a great understanding of the needs of your student - to be able to communicate and articulate your knowledge in such a way that you can impart to them your passion for dance.

I love the precision of a well-tuned team. I really enjoy watching a dance become tighter and tighter and all 8 dancers becoming one as movements begin to gel. It often causes the hair to stand on the back of my neck.

I also love that not every team dancer has to be an incredible solo dancer. It's a well known fact that great solo dancers don't automatically make great team dancers. I love that teaching ceili to a high standard gives every dancer the chance to be a World Champion.

**What sets good teams apart from great teams?** Dedication. You must be committed to working 100% as part of the team. It's no good making half the practices - a team needs to be unbelievably dedicated to succeed.

# Jason Hays

 **WORLD CHAMPION | NORTH AMERICAN NATIONAL CHAMPION ALL IRELAND CHAMPION | REGIONAL CHAMPION**

What I love most about Irish dancing is the feeling of home I get. It's comforting, relaxing and will always be there when you want it.

There is not friendship quite like the ones you have in Irish dancing. Your friends are there to celebrate in wins, losses, long practices, sore muscles and feet, but they stick it out with you the whole way.

"And those who were seen dancing were thought to be insane by those who could not hear the music" - Friedrich Nietzsche. I love this quote because I feel it captures everything about dance in general. Dance is something that does come from within, that is a force that wants be shared and celebrated, and most dances are created for those reasons too. To share and celebrate, as well as to pass on traditions and history.

> *A great dancer is someone who is working outside of practice by themselves, giving it their all in regular practice, and are always looking at ways to be better and better.*

A good dancer is someone who attends class, but does not push themselves both in and outside practice. They dance decently, place well (if they're lucky), but generally lack any drive to be better. A great dancer is someone who is working outside of practice by themselves, giving it their all in regular practice and are always looking at ways to be better and better. It comes back to having a drive to push yourself past your limits to create a new limit for yourself that you can continue to push further. Great dancers understand that defeat will happen, and even though it hurts and you may shed a few tears, they are already planning their next competition and they plan on working to place better.

**What does 'stage presence' mean to you?**

So I feel that it is more than just a look, or a glance, or a flick of your hair, but it is a whole presence or aura about you that tells the judges and audience, "I am here to dance my best and to show you why I deserve to win." It is a look of confidence, not cockiness, that makes many dancers so great to watch, because they have that look about them that makes you want to watch only them.

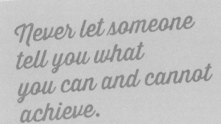

*Never let someone tell you what you can and cannot achieve.*

**Can you describe the feeling when you lift that globe?**

It is more a feeling of acknowledgement to me because, just like every Irish dancer out there, it is hours of hard work and commitment to become the best and being rewarded with a first place is such a rich feeling because you feel that all your work has paid off. It is exciting to win, but knowing that the blisters, cuts, soreness, hours and hours working on one step was the right combination of things because when you were onstage dancing your heart out, the judges believed that you were the best and danced the best.

# Declan McHale  ENGLAND

I would always start school at 9am but would always wake up at 7am every morning to allocate an hour's worth of practice before school, and I'd do the same after school too. This would be on top of the 4 classes I'd do midweek and the 6 hour workshops during the weekend. Irish dancing was my life and still is!

"The best thing for you to do is to do it over and over again!" Repetition of any trick, movement, step, or dance would always make me progress with what I was doing. I remember at one class Danny sent me away to do 100 straight leg clicks, because I forgot to lift up behind once. I learnt my lesson, and didn't forget to pick up again!

"I do not try to dance better than anyone else. I only try to dance better than myself." - Mikhail Baryshnikov

> "The best thing for you to do is to do it over and over again!"

I feel that it is hard to develop stage presence. To some people it is very natural and is all part and parcel of the environment they have grown up in; others can get up on the World stage and look like a bag of nerves even though they are totally confident and have danced fantastic.

**Can you describe the feeling when you lift that globe as a World Champion?**

It was, without a doubt, the best feeling in the world! (Excuse the pun.) Honestly, it was a fantastic feeling, and it was even better when Danny Doherty would come on stage for his teacher's award with a smile beaming from ear to ear. The thing that made winning the World even more special, was that my Grandmother always said I was going to be a World Champion from an early age, but unfortunately she never witnessed it. So, I gave a gift of one of my World gold medals to my Granddad before he was buried. Thanks to them both for having faith and looking down on me.

# Cathal Keaney

 IRELAND

Don't change who you are just to fit in - be different, try new things and push the boundary of what is being done at the moment. "Change the game, don't let the game change you." –Macklemore

*Growing up I always looked up to my brother in dancing as he is a 5 times world champion and taught me a lot.*

Stage presence never meant much to me so I never thought about it. I always felt in competitions that the judges were there to judge my dancing, not how I stood or walked on stage. I would always walk on stage relaxed with my arms swinging by my side. My teachers often gave out to me for it but I was never into the whole stiff arm fake smile walk on, it just wasn't me. Just be yourself is my advice, don't over-think the little things. Let your dancing show them what you can do.

Before going on stage at a big competition or performance I would always take three deep breaths, bless myself, and hit my legs a few times to get the blood pumping. This is something I always do and has become a bit of a habit.

Lifting the globe at the worlds is the best feeling ever. I remember winning my first worlds; it was amazing as I had been second 5 times to different people the previous few years. I finally got my chance to lift the globe and it's a truly amazing experience. Never give up on your dream is my advice. Keep fighting and doing your thing - when you get there it will be all the sweeter.

# Fergal Keaney

  IRELAND

I love the athleticism of Irish dancing, how a sub 2 minute dance can take so much energy and concentration. The precise choreography that takes hours to perfect. Finally, how Irish dancing moves are flavoured by each dancer's style - every dancer executes a move differently.

Before I go on stage I mentally go over all my steps and dances in my head. I visualise every part of the stage that I am going to hit after each turn and change of direction. I go over my tricks in slow motion visualising every smallest detail that I can. Then I smack my legs to get the blood flowing to them, swing my arms to feel big and walk on stage.

Stage presence is about not thinking about or caring about what other people think of you. Not thinking about what the judges think. It's about being more comfortable on stage than anywhere else in the world at that moment.

# Amanda Probert

**WORLD MEDAL HOLDER | NORTH AMERICAN NATIONAL CHAMPION
REGIONAL CHAMPION**

Not only do I love performing my solos onstage, but performing in a team makes dance even more enjoyable! The Claddagh teams spend a great deal of time together, and we have a lot of fun. It is nice to practice and travel with your best friends!

The best piece of advice I have ever been given is that when you compete, pretend you are performing and put on a show without holding back! When you walk on the stage, you need to dance like you own the stage! No matter how bad your day is going, or even if you messed up onstage, always put on a big smile and fly across the floor! Own the stage and never let anyone take that away from you!

"It's not about beating certain competitors, it is about achieving your goal." I am actually not sure where I heard that quote, or what the exact words are, but it was somewhere along those lines. Many dancers enter a competition with the mindset of beating another girl, rather than focusing on the actual goal. I have been a victim of this before, and I found that even though I had placed ahead of the competitor I wanted to, we both placed so poorly! Many dancers think like that, and don't realize what their actual goals are. Dancing should always be about yourself, how well you dance, and what your dancing looks like, not how your competitors dance.

I would have to say that reel is my favorite. I love how it is so fast and sharp! Once you start dancing your reel, there are no pauses. It is almost all running. For me, reel is the only dance where I feel like I'm truly flying through the air when I dance. I love performing it because everything is bigger and more exciting.

# Maggie Darlington

**WORLD CHAMPION | ALL IRELAND CHAMPION
NORTH AMERICAN NATIONAL CHAMPION | REGIONAL CHAMPION**

I love that Irish dancing is fast paced. As a kid I couldn't sit still and did everything quickly. I would change my clothes in 30 seconds, or scale the stairs as fast as possible. I also loved tricks. So, Irish dancing was the perfect combination of speed and intricacy for me.

"It's kind of fun to do the impossible." –Walt Disney

I think one of the most inspiring things is that everyone has different strengths, not just in dancing but in real life as well. I find other people's strengths inspire me to do things or to think in a way that I may otherwise not have come up with on my own. You can learn something from everyone and apply it or not apply it however you like to you and your life.

**Don't ever be afraid to fall on your behind!**

My favorite dance is slip jig. I love the elegance of a slip jig. To me it has a real personality. It's slow yet quick: graceful yet powerful. There is just something about a slip jig that excites me.

★ WORLD MEDAL HOLDER | REGIONAL CHAMPION ★

My favorite things about Irish dancing are upholding and expressing my Irish heritage and culture. When I dance I love creating something beautiful, artistic, athletic, and unique. I also absolutely love traditional Irish music and dancing to live musicians is so inspirational!

I am motivated because Irish dancing is ever changing and there is always something new to master and practice. I am also motivated to practice because I know that it takes a lot of hard work and many hours to shape and create a masterpiece.

Don't ever be afraid to learn! Be eager to learn as much as you can from teachers, dancers, and judges through their comments and corrections. Don't get discouraged by a bad day or criticism, but rather use it to propel yourself forward in your quest to be the best dancer possible! Always know that you can never stop improving.

*"Always remember that you are bigger than you believe, stronger than you seem, and smarter than you think." - Winnie the Pooh*

Stage presence for me is how I connect with the audience and take them on a journey through my dancing. I show them through my carriage and expression how much I love dancing. Stage presence captures the audience and tells them about who you are and how hard you worked to be there. It also creates an environment that allows my dancing and the music to paint an effortless masterpiece.

# Jan Gaca  ENGLAND

I'm not going to lie, sometimes practice is the hardest thing to do. It can be the last thing you want to do, I even have done my homework before I practised. But it is just imperative that you do it. I think about my goals and where I want to see myself standing when the results come out. If I want to be looking out from the top box and smiling or if I want to be looking up at someone else in first place. That's what really motivates me to practise. No matter how good you are dancing, you can always improve. So why not practise?

*Nothing is impossible, just believe in yourself and practise, and you can do anything.*

"There is no such thing as 'I can't', only 'I won't'." This is something my dancing teacher Hilary Joyce Owens has said to me for the past 20 years whenever I told her I couldn't do something she wanted me to do. However much I hated hearing it, now I know it to be true and have in part said it to other people.

Believe in yourself. Don't think that you don't deserve to win, no matter how many friends you dance against. If you have worked hard and you dance well, believe that you can do it. Also, dance as best and as hard as you can at class as well as at home. There is no point in dossing when your teacher looks away as you are only kidding yourself. Don't be embarrassed that other people in your class might think you're not cool. They're not cool! Try your best and you will be rewarded at competitions.

Stage presence means that you are confident in yourself as a dancer. You can command the stage and draw the attention of the audience without being aggressive. It is that something extra that attracts you to a dancer; more than technical ability or how sparkly the costume is. It's the flair or a passion that exudes from a dancer.

Can you describe the feeling when you lifted that globe at the World Championships?

I don't think I could describe the feeling. Although it took longer than the presentation for it to sink in that I had won the World Championships. It was immense shock. Not that I didn't think that I was able to or 'in the running' to win but after dancing for so long I couldn't believe I had finally done it, and lifted the globe. I was happy for my nan, my parents, my teacher, my brother, for me. I was delighted and thrilled and wish the same success to all who dare to try and claim it.

There are so many people who helped make this book possible!

Our incredible photographer Milton Baar, who kept his sense of humour intact while running all over the Convention Centre in Boston to photograph everyone.

Kathleen Downey, a talented young photographer who captured the amazing leap of Theresa Shaw that we are proud to use on our cover and as our logo.

Jimmy McNulty, John Egan from Feispix, and Tom Gregory from Shamrock Photo, all of whom graciously lent their images and passion for Irish dance to help fill in some photography gaps.

Our amazing designer Lisa from Idea Stylist, who brought our vision to life.

All of the dancers and teachers involved for sharing your words of wisdom so eloquently.

All of the parents of the dancers involved - you should all be very proud.

Our wonderful mothers, Narelle and Marie, for all their years curling our hair, sitting at competitions, and encouraging us to keep trying.

Our patient fathers, Peter and Michael, for putting up with the years of tears and tantrums.

Our better halves, Chris and Dirk, for understanding the long nights spent putting this baby together. Thank you!

P.S. I CAME 6TH! (You know who you are, and we'll never let you live it down!)


www.facebook.com/paradeofchampionsbook

www.instagram.com/paradeofchampions

www.paradeofchampions.tumblr.com

www.twitter.com/irishdance

www.paradeofchampionsbook.com

# Photo credits

All images in this book were taken by Milton Baar, MediaImages unless specified below

Page 7 Brogan McCay action shot - Jimmy McNulty

Page 9 Kevinah Dargan & Fiona Dargan - courtesy of Shamrock Photo

Page 16 Siobhan Casey large image - Jimmy McNulty

Page 16 Frances Dunne - supplied

Page 16 Frances Dunne & Siobhan Casey - Jimmy McNulty

Page 17 Nadine Martin action shot - Jimmy McNulty

Page 20 Rohan Bole action shot - Jimmy McNulty

Page 22 Alana Pearson - supplied

Page 23 Caroline Gray - courtesy of Shamrock Photo

Page 28 Tanya Cunningham - Jimmy McNulty

Page 30, 31 Craig Ashurst - supplied

Page 34, 35 Ayres family - supplied

Page 38 Garrett Coleman - supplied

Page 39 Layla Healy action shot - Jimmy McNulty

Page 40 Mona Ni Rodaigh - Jimmy McNulty

Page 41 Dearbhla Lennon - Jimmy McNulty

Page 41 Ciara Lennon, Mona Ni Rodaigh, and Dearbhla Lennon - courtesy of Feispix

Page 44 Declan McHale - supplied

Page 45 Cathal Keaney - image on right, supplied

Page 45 Fergal Keaney - supplied

Page 46 Maggie Darlington - Tim Allen Photography

Page 48 Jan Gaca - supplied

Made in the USA
Middletown, DE
06 December 2019